CHRISTMAS FUTURE

A PROPHECY

GOOD NEWS OF GREAT JOY!

BEN R PETERS

Christmas Future
@2023 by Ben R. Peters

Author grants permission for any non-commercial reproduction to promote the Kingdom of God. All rights reserved.

Published by
Kingdom Sending Center
P.O. Box 25
Genoa, IL 60135

www.kingdomsendingcenter.org
ben.peters@kingdomsendingcenter.org

Print edition ISBN: 9798866291090

All scripture quotations, unless otherwise indicated, are taken from the New King James Version ©1982 by Thomas Nelson, Inc. Used by permission. All rights reserved.

Cover design by Jess Seiler.

ACKNOWLEDGEMENTS

My heart is filled with great gratitude to those who have contributed so much towards the publishing of this book.

1. The Father, Son, and Holy Spirit, along with the Bible, and the more than seventy years of friendship, from which I have been blessed with gifts and talents that I didn't deserve.

2. My God-fearing, faith-filled parents and family, who taught me so much about hearing God's voice and walking in obedience to that voice.

3. My beautiful and loving wife Brenda, who is my partner in everything we do. She still has grace to give me time alone to write articles and books, when she'd rather be doing something together with me.

4. Carole Robbins, along with her husband Bruce, my amazing editing and publishing team, who love and serve God with all their hearts. They have quickly learned how to navigate Amazon's publication requirements, and I don't know what I'd do without them.

5. Jessica Seiler, whom we adopted as a spiritual daughter many years ago, is a computer graphics professional. She has put together two gorgeous book covers for me, including this one. I am so grateful for her and her dedication to our Lord Jesus Christ.

CONTENTS

	PREFACE	1
CHAPTER 1	AWAY IN A MANGER, O LITTLE TOWN OF BETHLEHEM	4
CHAPTER 2	HARK! THE HERALD ANGELS SING, ANGELS FROM THE REALMS OF GLORY	12
CHAPTER 3	WHILE SHEPHERDS WATCHED THEIR FLOCKS BY NIGHT	22
CHAPTER 4	WE THREE KINGS, STAR OF THE EAST	34
CHAPTER 5	SILENT NIGHT, O HOLY NIGHT	50
CHAPTER 6	JOY TO THE WORLD	60
CHAPTER 7	O COME, O COME EMMANUEL	70

PREFACE

Most people have read the book or seen the movie "A Christmas Carol" by Charles Dickens. In this story, a man named Ebenezer Scrooge is visited on Christmas Eve by the ghost of his deceased partner Jacob Marley, who warns him that three more ghosts will appear to him that night. The first was the Ghost of Christmas Past; the second, the Ghost of Christmas Present; and the third, the Ghost of Christmas Yet to Come.

The story came to a very happy conclusion. Tiny Tim, a delightful but sick and crippled young boy was greatly blessed by Scrooge, along with his father and family, by the previously grouchy and stingy miser. Scrooge had learned very valuable lessons from the visitations by the four ghosts on Christmas Eve.

The message of this book may actually have some common threads with "A Christmas Carol." However, we will see a much bigger and more wonderful picture of God's goodness and mercy, as we unveil the glorious possibilities and promises spoken through the prophets and God's Word of the Christmas Future. To the best of my knowledge, neither have used the term "Christmas Future."

In our previous book, "The Glorious Return of King Jesus," we shared Jesus' journey into Jerusalem for what would be His final Passover on earth. This was a subtle preview of His "Second Coming" journey from Heaven into Jerusalem to establish His glorious Kingdom. Even so, I believe that His original coming to earth, when he was born of a virgin in Bethlehem, was a subtle preview of what is going to happen on earth before His triumphant return to planet earth with the sound of the last trumpet and the voice of the Archangel.

Now this is where you come in. Will you also gladly and willingly say, like Mary said to Gabriel, "Let it be unto me according to Your word?" Are you willing to be an earthly vessel to birth the Christ child into the world around you? Are you willing to be like the Wise Men and follow the star to your Bethlehem? Are you willing to respond to angelic messengers, like the shepherds, and behold the future King of Israel in a manger? If your answer is yes, and you love Christmas and the Christ of Christmas, then you're going to love what Christmas Future holds for you!

Away in a Manger

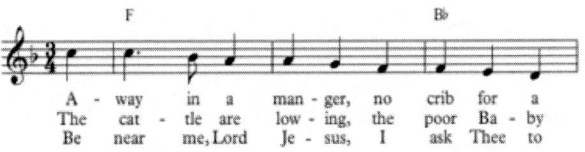

O Little Town Of Bethlehem

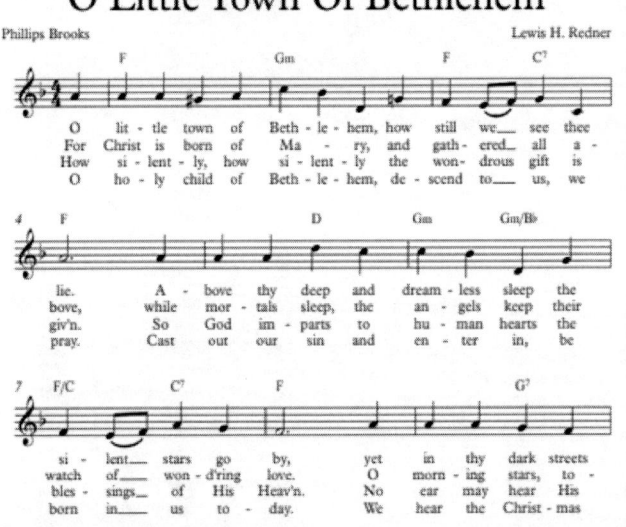

CHAPTER ONE

AWAY IN A MANGER, O LITTLE TOWN OF BETHLEHEM

"Location, location, location!" is the mantra of real estate agents. So, if you are Father God in Heaven, sending Your beloved Son into the world on a mission to save it, where would you send Him? Would you have chosen a lowly manger in the stable of a small farming town outside of Jerusalem, the royal city of Israel? Probably not! But God wasn't making a mistake, and He won't make a mistake placing you where He wants you either.

Do you ever feel like the "Inn" was too full for you, and you had to get your start with some less than human characters who smelled a lot like manure? Did you ever think God made a mistake in placing you where you felt less than the least, when you should have been given a place of greater honor? We probably have all felt that way at some point in our lives. If only we could be recognized for who we truly are! It feels like such a travesty that our great gifts and talents are being totally ignored by the people who should know better.

Well, welcome to the world of our awesome King Jesus! And be encouraged! In spite of such a humble beginning, God sent some special messengers to Jesus, Joseph, and Mary, letting let them know they were not forgotten. In God's perfect timing, Jesus would be recognized by many people, and He would powerfully fulfill His earthly destiny.

As we meditate on the entirety of the Christmas story, we need to see ourselves in this story. We must truly become a very important character in the plot of this great and glorious event we are calling Christmas Future. Let's take a quick look at the characters involved in that first Christmas drama in Bethlehem:

1. Baby Jesus
2. Mother Mary
3. Husband Joseph
4. Gabriel
5. Heavenly Hosts
6. Shepherds
7. Wise Men
8. King Herod
9. Ceasar Augustus
10. Zacharias the Priest
11. Wife Elizabeth
12. John the Baptist
13. Simeon
14. Anna

Christmas Future

You may already see one of the above characters as someone with whom you identify or emulate in the Christmas Future drama. We'll be interacting with most, if not all, of these characters in the chapters ahead, but let's focus first on that manger and the "Little Town of Bethlehem."

To bring about your Christmas Future, Jesus once again needs a manger in a humble stable, where only those in tune with the Spirit realm will actually recognize Him for Who He is. Jesus is asking you today, "Are you willing to become that humble, seemingly set-aside, feeding trough where I can rest?"

Do you feel you're too important for that? Or do you feel like Paul, who said he was the "chief among sinners," unworthy of the apostolic calling on his life. The main purpose of the manger at the Bethlehem Inn was most likely to feed the animals brought there by its patrons, such as the donkeys or horses they rode or that carried their burdens. It also could have been used to feed the owner's animals, as businesses usually operated out of residences in biblical times, and most families had animals that provided either milk, eggs, or transportation, etc.

I find the manger concept extremely significant and very applicable to our walk with God and the preparation for our Christmas Future. But before we discuss the significance of the manger, let's be a bit more specific and ask the obvious question. What does the term "Christmas Future" mean?

CHRISTMAS FUTURE

Christmas Future is the largely unheralded coming of Jesus in various ways into our humble world. This is not to be confused with His grand and glorious return. The sound of the trumpet and the voice of the Archangel will be heard when He establishes His earthly millennial reign.

Christmas Future is the prophetic promise that Jesus will show up in unexpected ways, impacting and changing the world through us, His body on the earth. He will once again shock the world, doing incredible and unexplainable miracles, like turning water into wine, raising the dead, walking on water, cleansing lepers, multiplying food, healing the sick and paralyzed, and setting free those who are bound by demons. While we have seen many of these miracles in small numbers, we're talking prophetically about an absolute explosion of signs, wonders, and miracles to capture the attention and headlines of the world's media outlets.

I would also call the Great Awakening Revival, which has already begun, a powerful part of Christmas Future. It will precede and prepare the way for the Second Coming of Jesus. It will get a lot of people excited about the ultimate return of the King of kings and Lord of lords and His Millennial Kingdom.

Christmas Future can happen in July or any month of the year, but I'm especially looking forward to celebrating Christmas Future, while most of the world is just celebrating Christmas Past. It will add a wonderful and very practical dimension to our joyful celebration.

Christmas Past was not the REALLY BIG EVENT. It was the birthing process leading up to the REALLY BIG EVENT, which was the crucifixion and resurrection of Jesus. And likewise, Christmas Future is not the REALLY BIG EVENT. It is the birthing process leading up to the REALLY BIG EVENT, which is the

Christmas Future

physical return of our Lord Jesus Christ and the establishment of His Kingdom on earth.

Christmas Past was a wonderful and important event, even if it wasn't as big as the finale thirty-three years later. Although Christmas Future isn't the biggest event, it is still important to God, and we don't want to miss it! We want to be aware of what God is doing and get excited about where Christmas Future is leading us. Lots of wonderful blessings will accompany this powerful event, getting us even more excited about the REALLY BIG EVENT that is yet to come.

THE MANGER

In Christmas Past, the host for Jesus' coming to earth was the innkeeper who also housed and fed various domestic animals, like Joseph's donkey. The same manger used as a feeding trough for these animals was filled with hay, which would have provided a comfortable resting place for the Baby Jesus.

The application for Christmas Future is that Jesus will be hosted by those who care for His people, including His prophetic intercessors, who bear His burdens. There will also be special rewards for the generous saints who provide for the needs of others who have made sacrifices to preach the gospel and serve others.

May we, as we look forward to our own Christmas Future, be good stewards of our resources, especially helping missionaries, evangelists, and those living by faith without any guaranteed income. Brenda and I have spent most of our adult lives living on the edge, by faith in God's provision. And we are eternally grateful to the many special friends who, without ever being asked for anything, have been prompted by the Holy Spirit to put some hay in our manger. I believe there are some special Christmas Future visits from the Son of God for each of them.

O LITTLE TOWN OF BETHLEHEM

What a beautiful, fitting picture we get from the name "Bethlehem," which literally means "House of Bread." In the book of Ruth, there came a time of famine when there was no bread in the House of Bread. It caused Elimelech and Naomi to migrate southeast to the land of Moab, where they could find food. After Naomi's husband and both sons died in Moab, she heard that there was once again bread in the House of Bread. Consequently, Naomi returned to Bethlehem with Ruth, her widowed daughter-in-law.

The prophetic type and shadow of this scenario is stunning. Jesus declared that He was the "Bread of Life." He was born in Bethlehem when there was a severe drought of spiritual bread in the land. The Jews were ruled by a combination of idolatrous Romans, proud scribes, and Pharisees, whom Jesus denounced as snakes and vipers who were headed for hell. Yes, there were some righteous priests such as Zacharias, the father of John the Baptist, but those who ruled over them did not provide any living bread to sustain their true spirituality.

Thus, Jesus came to restore spiritual bread to the Jewish people. And very appropriately, He made his first appearance in the Little Town of Bethlehem - the House of Bread.

As we are now Christ's body on the earth, we are also called to be living bread for the hungry around us. We can be that "Little Town of Bethlehem" to the hungry hearts in our world by

Christmas Future

choosing to partake of the Living Bread and then becoming what we eat. That's the picture we find in:

I Corinthians 10:17:
"For we, though many, are one bread and one body, for we all partake of that one bread."

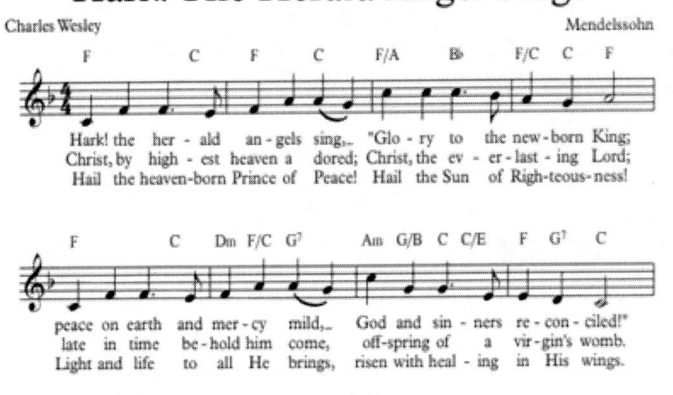

CHAPTER TWO

HARK! THE HERALD ANGELS SING, ANGELS FROM THE REALMS OF GLORY

If Christmas Future is going to resemble Christmas Past, we can surely expect a lot of angelic activity. And that is exactly what is now happening and what many prophetic voices have been proclaiming.

The Archangel Gabriel is the special envoy from Heaven's throne room, bringing the most important news to the most unsuspecting individuals on earth. Matthew didn't record the name of the "Angel of the Lord" who appeared in a dream to the Wise Men or to the shepherds in the field, and to Joseph on three separate occasions. But because of the importance of these messages, we can justifiably speculate that it was Gabriel. Luke, on the other hand, records that it was indeed the angel, Gabriel, who visited both the priest Zacharias and the virgin Mary.

The visit to Zacharias included the promise of a wonderful miracle, in that both the father and mother of John were quite old and past the time of childbearing. It was such a shock to Zacharias that he unwisely questioned such a declaration. He was then rebuked by Gabriel and told that he would be mute until the baby was born. It's hard to condemn the old priest, since it would require a miracle that hadn't happened since the days of Abraham and Sarah. Miracles in Israel had been infrequent the past several hundred years. As we mentioned in the previous chapter, Israel had been going through a very long spiritual drought.

However, the miracle of John's birth would pale in comparison to the miracle Gabriel promised the virgin Mary, who was what we would call "engaged" to the carpenter Joseph. Gabriel explained how she would be the recipient of the seed of God, Himself, and would have a child without a physical relationship with a human male.

Let's take a look at the dialogue between Gabriel and the virgin Mary in Luke 1:26-38. Let the Holy Spirit make some personal applications as you read this passage. If you were Mary hearing the words of Gabriel, how would you respond? This is for us guys as well. Remember, although none of us men can literally do what Mary did, you can certainly be a willing vessel, carrying Jesus in your heart and revealing Him to those in your sphere of influence.

Luke 1:26-27:
"Now in the sixth month the angel Gabriel was sent by God to a city of Galilee named Nazareth to a virgin betrothed to a man whose name was Joseph, of the house of David. The virgin's name was Mary."

Christmas Future

Luke 1:28:
"And having come in, the angel said to her, 'Rejoice, highly favored one, the Lord is with you; Blessed are you among women.'"

Luke 1:29:
"But when she saw him, she was troubled at his saying, and considered what manner of greeting this was."

Luke 1:30-33:
"Then the angel said to her, 'Do not be afraid, Mary, for you have found favor with God. And behold, you will conceive in your womb and bring forth a Son, and shall call His name Jesus. He will be great, and will be called the Son of the Highest; and the Lord God will give Him the throne of His father David. And He will reign over the house of Jacob forever, and of His Kingdom there will be no end.'"

Luke 1:34:
"Then Mary said to the angel, 'How can this be, since I do not know a man?'"

Luke 1:35-37:
"And the angel answered and said to her, 'The Holy Spirit will come upon you, and the power of the Highest will overshadow you; therefore, also, that Holy One who is to be born will be called the Son of God. Now indeed, Elizabeth your relative has also conceived a son in her old age; and this is now the sixth month for her who was called barren. For with God nothing will be impossible.'"

Luke 1:38:

"Then Mary said, 'Behold the maidservant of the Lord! Let it be to me according to your word.' And the angel departed from her."

What a privilege and honor it was for Mary to literally give birth to the Son of God! Yet Jesus humbled Himself in a very profound way and chose to refer to Himself as the "Son of Man." But you and I also have the privilege and honor to carry Jesus and present Him to everyone we possibly can through the anointing of His Holy Spirit.

WHO WERE JOSEPH AND MARY?

I have a confession to make. As often as I've read through the Bible, I have never paid much attention to the genealogies recorded in Matthew and Luke, except to notice that they went back to Abraham in Matthew and all the way back to Adam in Luke. It was a significant revelation to me that I hadn't noticed how both records give us the genealogy of Joseph and neither tell us about Mary's genealogy.

Since Joseph was not the biological father of Jesus, but Mary was the biological mother, it would seem more important to give us Mary's genealogy than Joseph's. However, both Mathew and Luke did just the opposite. While meditating upon this information, I felt that God wanted to share some important truths with us before Christmas Future gets into full celebration mode.

1. Joseph, for all practical purposes, adopted Jesus as His own Son. Even though he was not the biological father,

Christmas Future

God recognized the adoption process as important enough to give us his genealogy in both Matthew and Luke, tracing him back to King David, Abraham, and Adam. I believe this is a beautiful picture of what happens when God adopts us or grafts us into His family. We inherit the genealogy, with all the rights and privileges, of our adoptive Father in Heaven. Just as Jesus was adopted by Joseph, a Son of David, and accepted the title of a "Son of David," through Jesus, we are adopted and also become spiritual Sons of David and of our Father God, Himself.

2. Mary, although highly honored by God through Gabriel, was not of the seed of David. She was most likely of the priestly tribe of Levi because we are told that she was a relative of Elizabeth, Zacharias' wife, a "daughter of Aaron" (Luke 1:5). In this marriage partnership, God united in Jesus the offices of Kings and Priests. What a beautiful prophetic picture of us! As Jesus was, we are called to be Kings and Priests unto God (Revelation 1:6, 5:10).

3. Mary, although of the priestly tribe of Levi, was unaccomplished, and an unworthy "maidservant" in her own eyes. According to her words in what is known as the "Magnificat" in Luke 1:46-55, Mary considered herself "lowly" in verses 48 and 52. She declares that God has rejected the "proud" but honors those who fear Him in humility. What an encouragement to all of us who feel quite insignificant and of very little value to God and His Kingdom! God usually choses the undervalued to accomplish great things for His Kingdom (I Corinthians 1:27-30).

4. Gabriel did not have the same expectations of the young virgin that he had of the elderly priest, Zacharias. He did not rebuke her for asking how this could be, since she wasn't in a physical relationship with any man. Gabriel understood how difficult this would be to comprehend. There had never been such a miracle recorded in the history of man, as opposed to the miracle of an older couple having a child as did Abraham and Sarah in their older years. My take on this fact is that God does expect more from those who have more knowledge and history with God. Remember, even Samuel was rebuked for "Looking on the outward appearance," whereas God always looks at the heart. Samuel had looked at David's older brothers as being great candidates for becoming the future king. He looked at their height and they reminded him of King Saul, but God said no to each of them and chose young David instead.

HOW TO GET PREGNANT WITH A "GOD ASSIGNMENT"

Perhaps my favorite verse quoted above is verse 35, where Gabriel explains how she will get pregnant. What a powerful verse! Let's look at it again.

Luke 1:35:
"And the angel answered and said to her, 'The Holy Spirit will come upon you, and the power of the Highest will overshadow you; therefore, also, that Holy One, who is to be born, will be called the Son of God.'"

This scenario immediately reminds me of at least two other accounts in Scripture. First, we can look at the Genesis creation account.

Genesis 1:2:
"The earth was without form and void; and darkness was on the face of the deep. And the Spirit of God was hovering over the face of the waters."

The word "hovering" could also be translated "brooding," like a bird incubating its eggs. It was preparing to birth something wonderful for every person to enjoy.

The second significant similar reference is found in the Book of Acts.

Acts 2:2-4:
"And suddenly there came a sound from heaven, as of a rushing mighty wind, and it filled the whole house where they were sitting. Then there appeared to them divided tongues, as of fire, and one sat upon each of them. And they were all filled with the Holy Spirit and began to speak with other tongues, as the Spirit gave them utterance."

All three of these passages are about the birthing of something wonderful and totally transformative, and they all involve the manifest presence of the Holy Spirit covering them in one way or another. The passage in Acts is about the birthing of the New Testament Church, or the Body of Christ, which would now have the power of the Holy Spirit to bring about the transformation of the world as they knew it.

EXTREMELY IMPORTANT APPLICATION

Don't miss this most valuable point. If you are small in your own eyes, a servant or handmaiden of the Lord; If you fear the

Lord and want to serve Him; If you feel like a failure as the disciples did in Jesus' day, but truly want to build His Kingdom; I have great news for you. That same Holy Spirit who brooded over the waters, hovered over Mary, later filled the house, and put fire on the heads of 120 disciples is very willing now to hover over you and impregnate you with the seed of something that will become far bigger than you. It's kind of like a 4'11" lady giving birth to a baby boy who grows up to be seven feet tall, which is a weak comparison at best. Jesus mentioned a better illustration about the tiny mustard seed, which has the potential to grow into a small tree.

All that is required of us is a strong desire to please and serve our Master, and a willingness to say "YES!" to whatever He asks us to do. As a result, we can definitely experience the presence of the Holy Spirit hovering over us. He will infuse a seed within us that can produce something far greater than our own capabilities. It is the power to bring about a Christmas Future into our own world, our own lives, our families, and our society.

MORE ABOUT ANGELIC ACTIVITY

From reports in recent years and from books like "Dreams and Visions" by Tom Doyle and Greg Webster, angelic activity has been on the rise to prepare people especially in "non-Christianized" nations for the Second Coming of Christ. This has been happening especially in the nations ruled by Islamic leaders. As in biblical times, many of these visitations happen in dreams and produce bold and powerful faith, even though that faith can mean certain death, often from family members.

In spite of persecution, the churches in some of these nations are the fastest growing in the world. They have begun to

Christmas Future

experience Christmas Future ahead of most of the western church. But God hasn't forgotten us either. He's probably just provoking us to jealousy.

Just like angels prepared shepherds and priests, etc., for Christmas Past, angels are now busily preparing us for Christmas Future. They're looking for the "Mary's" that will respond like she did, presenting themselves as humble servants of the Most High God.

Speaking of angels and shepherds, let's now shift our focus to their interaction with each other in Christmas Past and what that means to us in Christmas Future.

♩ = 120
♩ = 120
Nahum Tate
While shepherds watched their flocks
Melody: T. Este
While shep - herds watched their flocks by night, all
"Fear not," said he (for might - y dread had
"To you in Da - vid's town this day is
"The heav'n - ly babe you there shall find to
Thus spake the ser - aph; and forth - with ap -
"All glo - ry be to God on high, and
4
seat - ed on the ground, the an - gel of the
seized their trou - bled mind); "glad ti - dings of great
born of Da - vid's line a sa - viour, who is
hu - man view dis - played, all mean - ly wrapped in
-peared a shi - ning throng of an - gels prais - ing
to the earth be peace; good - will hence - forth from
7
Lord came down, and glo - ry shone a - round.
joy I bring to you and all man - kind.
Christ the Lord; and this shall be the sign:
swath - ing bands, and in a man - ger laid."
God, who thus ad - dressed their joy - ful song:
heav'n to men be - gin and ne - ver cease."
This edition Andrew Sims 2014

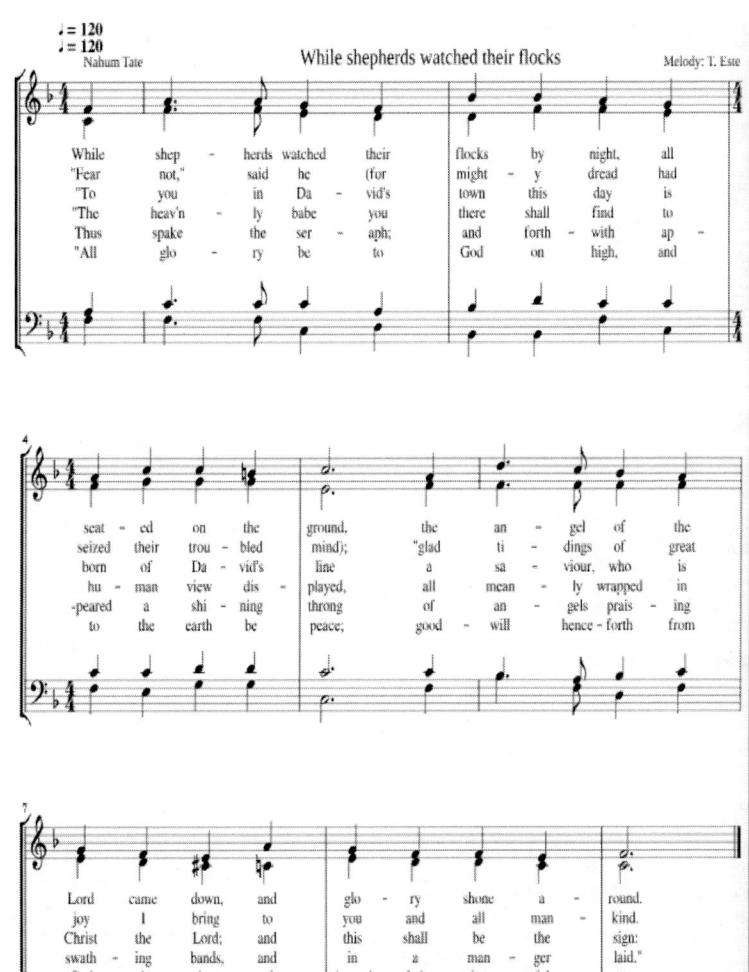

CHAPTER THREE

WHILE SHEPHERDS WATCHED THEIR FLOCKS BY NIGHT

Shepherds have always been an essential part of the Christmas Past story. What we want to discover is how they fit into Christmas Future. This is their story from the book of Luke:

Luke 2:8-9:
"Now there were in the same country shepherds living out in the fields, keeping watch over their flock by night. And behold, an angel of the Lord stood before them, and the glory of the Lord shone around them, and they were greatly afraid."

Luke 2:10-12:
"Then the angel said to them, 'Do not be afraid, for behold I bring you good tidings of great joy which will be to all people. For there is born to you this day in the city of David a Savior,

who is Christ the Lord. And this will be the sign to you: You will find a Babe wrapped in swaddling cloths, lying in a manger.'"

Luke 2:13-14:
"And suddenly there was with the angel a multitude of the heavenly host, praising God and saying: 'Glory to God in the highest, and on earth peace, goodwill toward men.'"

What a beautiful story from Christmas Past! The symbolism is quite amazing and powerful. It's a story that connects our previous chapter on angels with this chapter about shepherds. It's a connection that provides us with great revelation, as we allow the Holy Spirit to enlighten our understanding, while anticipating Christmas Future.

Let's focus on the angelic activity first. We'll start with "an angel of the Lord" appearing to the shepherds, who was most likely Gabriel. When the angel had concluded his message to the shepherds, the night sky was suddenly filled with a great "multitude of the heavenly hosts."

I love this picture as I visualize it in my mind. It just appears to be one powerful angel, but that one angel was enough to scare the daylights out of these startled shepherds. However, there were a lot more angelic beings present than what met their eyes. Suddenly, they are surrounded by hosts of angels. The word "host" in the Greek simply means army. So now, instead of just one bright and shiny heavenly being, they are seeing the army of Heaven praising God and saying, *"Glory to God in the Highest, and on earth, peace, goodwill toward men"* (Luke 2:14). What an amazing experience!

Christmas Future

In II Kings 6:17, we read that Elisha could see, in the Spirit, the army of Heaven as well. His servant was unable to see them until Elisha asked God to open his spiritual eyes. Then his servant was no longer afraid of the Syrian army; he could see that there were more for them than against them.

The application that I see from these stories is that God has myriads of angels to do His bidding. Consequently, when we need a little angelic assistance, they are plentiful and available. There will always be more for us than against us. Perhaps that's part of the context of this passage:

Romans 8:31:
"What then shall we say to these things, if God is for us, who can be against us?"

As usual, the "angel of the Lord" understood the fright of the poor shepherds and tried to calm their fears with a "Fear not!" Then he gave them valuable information and instructions about how to respond to this incredible event, which is typical of angelic visitations. Angels don't normally appear just to chat about the weather or our favorite hobby; they always have a purpose when they manifest.

Now, let's transition from the angels to the shepherds.

Luke 2:8:
"Now there were in the same country shepherds living out in the fields, keeping watch over their flock by night."

IN THE SAME COUNTRY

This little prepositional phrase "in the same country" doesn't seem too important. However, many years ago, I remember being up early in the morning, driving down the highway to our next ministry appointment, and this simple phrase started repeating itself in my mind. Since I couldn't read and drive at the same time, I began quoting familiar Scriptures for my morning meditation. Somehow, I started quoting the familiar Christmas story verses from Luke 2, until I came to verse eight, and that first statement caught my attention. *"There were in the same country, shepherds . . ."* These shepherds were physically located in the same region as Joseph, Mary, and Baby Jesus. As I meditated, it began to take on a special significance. They just happened to be watching their sheep close to where Jesus was born. They just happened to be out in the fields, and they most likely spent their night outside around a campfire for warmth and to keep their sheep safe from predators. Why is that significant?

In every language, that I'm familiar with, other than English, the word "shepherd" is the same as "pastor." I served as "pastor" for almost 30 years, mostly as the founding pastor of a small-town church. These Bethlehem shepherds/pastors were not living in luxury, nor sleeping on lovely memory foam beds. Because of their love for their sheep, like our Great Shepherd, they were willing to sacrifice their comfort. They were sleeping under the stars, keeping their vulnerable sheep safe from predators that would readily feast on fresh mutton, if given the opportunity.

Being "in the same country" (close by or in the same region), spoke to me of Christian leaders being in the same place spiritually where God was birthing something new and special. They didn't distance themselves from revivals because they weren't the style of revival that they preferred or were familiar with. They weren't proud and haughty like the Pharisees who never accepted the idea that their Messiah could be born in a barn and laid in a manger. These were truly humble pastors with a desire to be close to Jesus in Christmas Past.

But now, as we begin to participate in Christmas Future, Jesus is being reborn in so many ways and in so many places. Will we be in the "same country?" As leaders, will we have the heart and mind to go and see what God has birthed in the current waves of revival and renewal? In my lifetime, there have been numerous revivals and moves of God that have touched millions. However, like in the days of Jesus, religious leaders are slow to embrace moves of God, finding ways to criticize them for anything they see as not totally Kosher. Even when the non-charismatic revival broke out recently at Asbury University, many religious leaders were quick to criticize, but thankfully many others were "in the same country" and hastened to see what God was doing.

KEEPING WATCH OVER THEIR FLOCKS BY NIGHT

Pastors who love their sheep don't prioritize their own luxurious living and comfort. They are not justifying their lavish lifestyle by preaching a lopsided gospel. They are not ignoring Jesus' teachings about laying down their lives and being willing to suffer, even taking up a cross to follow Him. Instead, they are gladly giving up personal comforts to keep their sheep safe, strong, and healthy. They may not have a huge flock to provide a luxurious lifestyle, but they have the satisfaction of knowing that they have been true and faithful to their calling.

Jesus made it clear in John 10 how important it was for a true shepherd to lay his life down for his sheep. Ezekiel 34 has many harsh words for shepherds who fleece their flock and feast on mutton, but don't properly care for their sheep. As a shepherd/pastor, I want to be known as one who was there for the sheep, serving them, rather than demanding that they serve me.

These shepherds were on duty both day and night. The life of a true pastor is not an easy life. They should receive honor, but they should also remember that they have a great example in Jesus, who came not to be served but to serve.

SHEPHERDS RESPOND TO CHRISTMAS PAST ANNOUNCEMENT

The account of the angelic encounter by the shepherds is given in Luke 2:15-20:

Luke 2:15:
"So it was, when the angels had gone away from them into heaven, that the shepherds said to one another, 'Let us now go to Bethlehem and see this thing that has come to pass, which the Lord has made known to us.'"

Luke 2:16:
"And they came with haste and found Mary and Joseph, and the Babe, lying in a manger."

Luke 2:17:
"Now when they had seen Him, they made widely known the saying which was told them concerning this Child."

Christmas Future

Luke 2:18:
"And all those who heard it marveled at those things which were told them by the shepherds."

Luke 2:19:
"But Mary kept all these things and pondered them in her heart."

Luke 2:20:
"Then the shepherds returned, glorifying and praising God for all the things that they had heard and seen, as it was told them."

Let's examine the first two of the verses recorded above:

Luke 2:15:
"So it was, when the angels had gone away from them into heaven, that the shepherds said to one another, 'Let us now go to Bethlehem and see this thing that has come to pass, which the Lord has made known to us.'"

Luke 2:16:
"And they came with haste and found Mary and Joseph, and the Babe, lying in a manger."

The shepherds, who were privileged to be "in the same country," wasted no time obeying the instructions that the angel had given them. They came "with haste." These "pastors" did not have theological reasons to not believe the Heavenly Messengers of Christmas Past. They did not have seminary degrees or any other ecclesiastical positions to make them hesitate. Instead, they hurriedly slipped away to be as close to their Messiah as possible. I believe these unnamed men are perfect examples of how to be true shepherds/pastors.

Luke 2:17:
"Now when they had seen Him, they made widely known the saying which was told them concerning this Child."

Luke 2:18:
"And all those who heard it marveled at those things which were told them by the shepherds."

What a perfect picture of pastors who also become evangelists! They cared for their sheep, but they also realized that God was enlarging their vision and their sphere of influence. I can't help but recall our own journey from being a local shepherd/pastor in a small town on the coast of Washington State for about fifteen years until God called us to leave home in a recreational vehicle and live on the road for five years with two young sons in tow. God had given us a message that He wanted us to share with His sheep in other places, including other countries.

Now, you may not see yourself as a pastor, because you don't lead a "local" church. But the term "pastor" has been misapplied in church circles. It really has more to do with your gifting to love, heal, and protect those who are weak or young in the faith than with leading a "church." Your pastoral ministry can be in your home, on your phone, on social media, etc. But if you're faithful on a small scale with the gifts God has given you, I believe God has more open doors for you to walk through. He wants to use you more than He ever has in the past. He wants you to be a vessel through which to birth Christmas Future in your world and sphere of influence.

Verse 18 says that those who heard the testimony of the shepherds "marveled" at their words. Who wouldn't marvel at

Christmas Future

the incredible things that the shepherds had declared to them? After all, these were simple, honest Israelites. They had no reputation for fabricating stories to make themselves feel important. They were not polished preachers, who knew how to enhance a story to emotionally influence their audience. They were humble shepherds who sacrificed a good night's sleep to keep their woolly friends safe at night. It was such an unbelievable story, but it was told in such a way, by such honest men, that it was totally believable.

Yes, these humble shepherds had an incredible encounter with heavenly visitors back in Christmas Past. But I would like for you to believe that God has some special heavenly encounters for you as well, as we move into Christmas Future and begin to prepare for the REALLY BIG EVENT, "The Glorious Return of King Jesus," as talked about in our book by that name.

Luke 2:19:
"But Mary kept all these things and pondered them in her heart."

Such a powerful verse, with so much application for us as we enter Christmas Future. I can only imagine how Mary felt and what went on in her heart having been visited by these shepherds, who gave their impassioned testimony of the mind-blowing events that had just occurred on the night watch in their field. Additionally, because of the awkwardness of her pregnancy situation, it's most likely that Mary had told very few people about her incredible encounter with the mighty archangel, Gabriel.

She must have had moments of being overwhelmed, thinking she was having a crazy dream. And now, the baby was born, and all her maternal instincts were activated with the single focus of taking care of her newborn son. Then came this unexpected divine interruption by a group of smelly shepherds telling her and Joseph about an unprecedented event. Mary had been visited by one powerful angel, but these shepherds talked about an army of angels and glorious worship they had heard with their own ears.

These humble shepherds had driven home the truth about her precious bundle, who was sleeping in that manger wrapped in swaddling clothes. She was not having a crazy dream. This baby was indeed the Son of God! It's not something she could tell all her friends and family about. They would look at her with strange looks and would be thinking, "Right, Mary, your little baby is the Son of God. And I'm the Roman Ceasar." What a unique situation she found herself in! What else could Mary do but keep everything to herself? She quietly and privately thanked God for the honor of giving birth to this precious child, who was the Creator of the World and also the future Redeemer of all mankind!

IMPORTANT APPLICATION

This may or may not seem obvious, but what an example the shepherds and Mary give us as we enter Christmas Future. Both were humble, non-celebrities in their world. They were both blessed by heavenly visitations, but they didn't try to make a name for themselves. They simply obeyed and made themselves available to God. Mary, especially, is an example of how we shouldn't boast or brag when God is using us. When God reveals something to us, we need to ponder in our hearts what to do with it, if He hasn't already told us. We need to die to the need to be known and famous. The shepherds and Mary

Christmas Future

both became well known for their roles in Christmas Past, although the names of these obedient shepherds/pastors were not given. God exalts the humble, and I know they are well known in Heaven, and some day we will meet them.

Finally, it's time to transition to another important group of Christmas Past characters. I know they have something very important to teach us about Christmas Future.

We Three Kings

John Henry Hopkins, Jr.

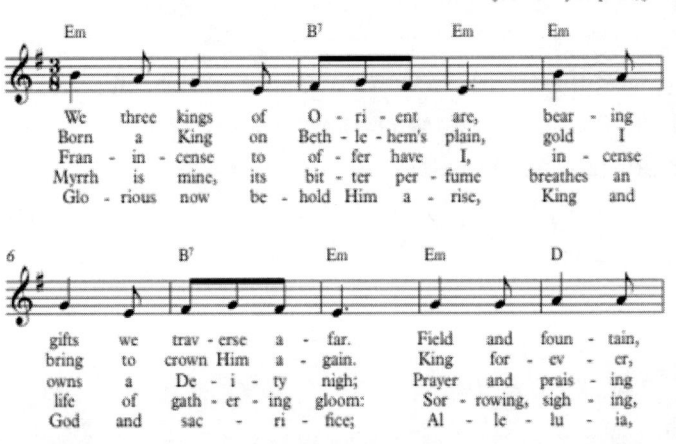

We three kings of O-ri-ent are, bear-ing
Born a King on Beth-le-hem's plain, gold I
Fran-in-cense to of-fer have I, in-cense
Myrrh is mine, its bit-ter per-fume breathes an
Glo-rious now be-hold Him a-rise, King and

gifts we trav-erse a-far. Field and foun-tain,
bring to crown Him a-gain. King for-ev-er,
owns a De-i-ty nigh; Prayer and prais-ing
life of gath-er-ing gloom: Sor-row-ing, sigh-ing,
God and sac-ri-fice; Al-le-lu-ia,

STAR OF THE EAST

Words by George Cooper
Music by Amanda Kennerch

Flowing Waltz

Star of the East, O Beth-le-hem's star,
Star of the East, un-dimmed by each cloud,

CHAPTER FOUR

WE THREE KINGS, STAR OF THE EAST

Truthfully, we have no idea how many "wise men" traveled from the east, following that very special star. The idea of "three wise men" or "magi," as they are also called, comes from the fact that they brought three different gifts: gold, frankincense, and myrrh.

The story recorded in Chapter 2 of Matthew is not easily understood by our western minds. We might question whether or not they were practicing astrology, which is something that we would consider from the dark side. We might also speculate about what that star really was. Some astronomers have claimed that it was an aligning of planets or stars, which made it look like an extra-large star.

Our objective is not to solve or give our opinion about these questions. We will leave that to those who specialize in solving these mysteries. Our intent is simply to see the prophetic and spiritual significance of these special men who traveled many miles for one purpose. They wanted to honor and worship "the King of the Jews." Let's look at Matthew's report regarding these important characters in the Christmas Past drama:

Matthew 2:1-2:
"Now after Jesus was born in Bethlehem of Judea in the days of Herod the king, behold, wise men from the East came to Jerusalem, saying, 'Where is He who has been born King of the Jews? For we have seen His star in the East and have come to worship Him.'"

These mysterious figures have great significance in the Christmas Past story, but they also have very incredible significance to our Christmas Future story. Let's investigate.

What a contrast with the shepherds we talked about in the previous chapter! These men were not "in the same country." They were from a far country in the East. They were most likely highly educated, and perhaps they understood the history of the Jews. However, they were probably not converts to Judaism, and possibly using some form of astrology. Perhaps they were similar to King Cyrus, who was not a Jew, but was used by God to bless the Jews. He does surprise us at times when He puts a special anointing, like a political anointing, on someone that the church would deem unusable by God.

These men were not lowly shepherds. They were called kings and magi. When they arrived in Jerusalem, they began to ask people where the new King was, probably assuming he had been born into the current royal family. Herod, who knew nothing about the "Babe in the Manger" story, called these wise men to him in a secret meeting, asking when they had first seen the star.

The Wise Men didn't actually visit the manger as we usually see in our Christmas pageants. They came later when Joseph and Mary lived in a house. No, they weren't poor. They were obviously quite wealthy, bringing gifts of gold, frankincense, and myrrh. Their gifts, it is speculated, provided the resources for Joseph and Mary to travel to Egypt to keep Jesus safe. They lived there until the death of Herod, the evil Jewish King who tried to kill Baby Jesus.

APPLICATION PLEASE!

So glad you asked! Paul said, *"Not many wise according to the flesh, not many mighty, not many noble, are called"* (I Corinthians 1:26b). He didn't say *not any;* He said *not many.* God is God and He can choose whomever He wishes, whenever He wishes. Sometimes He wants to use the wealth or power of a man or woman to do special things that a poor man or woman may not be positioned to accomplish. God certainly used a number of emperors or "kings of kings" to make His name known in the days of Joseph, and also Daniel and his three Hebrew companions in their times.

Please don't feel left out if you only have a modest amount of wealth or power. As long as you humble yourself like these Wise Men did, and you don't esteem yourself too highly but instead give God the glory, then God desires to use you greatly!

As mentioned above, God can also choose to use those who don't really know Him, like King Cyrus. He even used the Chief Priest to prophesy about Jesus, although he wasn't a believer in Jesus. He prophesied from his official position, not his personal opinion.

But what I love about these Wise Men is their tenacity, commitment, perseverance, and passion to find this newborn King. Notice their responses when the special star reappeared and when they came into the house where Jesus was.

Matthew 2: 9:
"When they heard the king, they departed; and behold, the star which they had seen in the East went before them, till it came and stood over where the young Child was."

Matthew 2:10:
"When they saw the star, they rejoiced with exceedingly great joy."

Matthew 2:11:
"And when they had come into the house, they saw the young Child with Mary His mother, and fell down and worshiped Him. And when they had opened their treasures, they presented gifts to Him; gold, frankincense, and myrrh."

These men from the East must have had some kind of heavenly encounter to be so tremendously passionate about seeing this child from Heaven. The angel told the shepherds that he was bringing them good tidings of great joy. In Matthew 2:10, we see that the Wise Men *"rejoiced with exceedingly great joy."* It sounds to me like they may have also heard from Heaven's angelic messengers.

Christmas Future

When they saw the young boy Jesus, they *"fell down and worshiped Him."* They were probably used to people bowing down to them, but when they saw Jesus, they fell down and worshiped Him. It was later reported that Jesus' younger brothers didn't even believe in Him for a time, but these strangers from afar had received a revelation from Heaven about His importance and significance. He was worthy of their absolute adoration and worship. May we all get that same revelation from our Father in Heaven!

Matthew 2:12:
"Then, being divinely warned in a dream that they should not return to Herod, they departed for their own country another way."

These Wise Men totally submitted to directions from above. Like the centurion in Matthew 8:5-10, they understood authority. They also had people under their authority who did whatever they were told. They all recognized Jesus as being the one over them, and they responded like they would expect their own servants to respond.

THE ANOINTING OF KINGS AND WISE MEN

These Magi from a far country are also known as "Wise Men" and "Kings," as often sung in the well-known Christmas carol "We Three Kings." In order to apply this fact to what we are calling "Christmas Future," I'd like to take a little space to share some thoughts on what it means to be a King and what it means to be a Wise Man.

In our earlier book "Kings and Kingdoms," we shared the revelation that in the centuries before and after the days of Jesus, there were many "kings of kings" who ruled over a vast amount of territory of the then-known world. All regional kings were under the authority of the emperor or the Caesar. Herod was such a king over the Jews in Jerusalem and Israel. The common people understood that concept which had been a part of their world for longer than they or their grandparents had lived.

Thus, when John the Revelator wrote twice that God had called us to be Kings and Priests in the Book of Revelation, the people understood. We had been given the privilege and responsibility to co-administrate the Kingdom of the King of kings and Lord of lords. It would have been a sobering thought to the readers of John's day.

Every king, sovereign or not, has certain responsibilities that go with his privileges, and this is what God has given to all of us. Sovereign despots and dictators can get away with almost anything, but a king, who is required to answer to a King of kings, must do the bidding of his Lord or suffer the consequences of his disobedience. Historically, that would not only be the end of his kingship, but the end of his life on this earth.

At the same time, the underling kings had many privileges. Herod was entitled to make and carry out certain decrees, which included killing all the male boys two years old and under. A later king, also with the name of Herod, had John the Baptist arrested, imprisoned, and later decapitated for pointing out sin in the royal family. If they didn't offend the Caesar, regional kings could wield that kind of power. They were also given the ability to tax the people, so they could live in some level of luxury.

APPLICATION

As we move into Christmas Future, we need to understand that God is calling us to function as kings under our King of kings.

1. Our first role is to seek Him, like the Wise Men, so we can truly worship Him. These Christmas Past kings made great sacrifices to behold His face, and then they fell down to worship Him. They weren't too proud to declare their submission to a small child, because they had been given a revelation from Heaven as to His greatness. They positioned themselves to become servant-kings under His Lordship.

2. Our second role is to give Him gifts revealing His worthiness. The kings from the East gave Him gifts of gold, frankincense, and myrrh, which He Himself had originally created to bless His people. Our Christmas Future gifts to King Jesus should include what we received from Him that has blessed us the most. I would suggest that our greatest wealth would be the spiritual gifts and talents that He has endowed us with. We should continuously present these gifts to Jesus, sincerely purposing their use for His glory and honor, and not our own. He will always give them back to us with a fresh anointing to accomplish more for His Kingdom.

    We can also present financial gifts to Him by giving to those who are building His Kingdom. I don't think these kings from the east carefully calculated a tithe of what they had. Instead, they focused on His worthiness and what they could give that appropriately revealed His worthiness. Our giving should be out of love, respect, and honor, rather than out of duty and a desire for personal blessing. Our hearts should desire to be as generous as possible to honor Him.

For those who don't have the faith to trust God with resources that they depend upon for their daily needs, God challenges them to test or prove Him in Malachi 3:10. The first reason for giving is "that there may be food in My house." In other words, your giving promotes and sustains His House or His Kingdom. Once again, we should remember that our spiritual gifts and talents are much more important to Him than our money, and He wants us to totally dedicate and surrender them to God.

3.   Our third role is to protect those we rule over. Kings were in charge of the safety and security of their subjects. As kings, we must watch over our people, like the shepherds watched over their sheep, to keep them safe.

4.   Our fourth role is to provide justice without favoritism or taking bribes. This was Solomon's first assignment as king. He had to function as the supreme court over all of Israel.

In America, and other western nations, there is a separation of powers with a separate justice system. When you have a king, the king makes the rules and executes justice for the most difficult cases.

5.   The fifth role of the king is to provide an opportunity for his subjects to prosper if they are willing to work hard. He

needs to administrate in such a way that the people have the resources to start and maintain farms and businesses.

With this extra little bit of information about being kings under our omnipotent King of kings, let's visualize how this affects Christmas Future for us.

First of all, there was a perfect time for the shepherds to come on the scene and offer their worship. It was appropriate that they showed up at the stable, the feeding place for domestic animals. They had just come from their own domestic animals and probably smelled a lot like the stable.

PERFECT TIMING

When the Wise Men from the East came, it was the appropriate time for them. They found the child in a house, probably very clean and sweet-smelling. They also came with financial assistance at the time that Joseph, Mary, and Jesus would need it for their travels to Egypt.

APPLICATION

God has the perfect time for you to be on the stage with Jesus, during this Christmas Future drama. You won't miss it if you keep a humble and willing heart. You will also enjoy that special time in His presence.

WISE MEN STILL SEEK HIM

Because these kings were also called "Wise Men," I will share what I believe the Holy Spirit is saying at this time:

- There is an unprecedented anointing of wisdom and the gift of wisdom coming upon those who seek the face of their King of kings in this upcoming season (which I call Christmas Future).

- When decisions have to be made, there will suddenly be someone in the group of leaders who will know exactly what to do. When trouble or confusion arises, or when the enemy stirs up controversy, the counsel of leaders will have an unusual unity of opinion and take decisive action.

- This wisdom will lead to many open doors for people, and they will become aware of the purpose of Christmas Future - to prepare them for the Really Big Event.

Finally, to end this specific discussion, let's remember that wisdom is both a special Gift of the Holy Spirit (I Corinthians 12:7), and it's also available to all members of the body of Christ as shared by James.

James 1:5:
"If any of you lacks wisdom, let him ask of God, who gives to all liberally and without reproach, and it will be given to him."

Throughout the book of Proverbs, Solomon reminds us of the importance of wisdom. Solomon asked God for wisdom and understanding because he was acutely aware that he would need them to rule over the people.

We should try to emulate Solomon's desire for wisdom because we definitely need it to navigate this confusing world we

Christmas Future

inhabit. In Christmas Future, wisdom will most certainly accompany God's visitation.

THE STAR

The star is the most mysterious part of this story. I personally have no fresh revelation as to what this star was or how the Wise Men discovered it. My best guess is that an angel appeared to them, perhaps in a dream, and told them they would see a new star in the sky, indicating that a prince had been born in Israel. Perhaps they were told that the star would move westward, bringing them to the birthplace of the future King of the Jews. Or perhaps they just saw a new star and understood they should travel to Jerusalem.

When a star appeared that they had never seen before, the Wise Men readied their camels for travel. After a long tiresome journey, they finally arrived in the nation of Israel. Entering the capital city of Jerusalem, they inquired about the birth of the new Jewish prince, so they could pay homage. When Herod heard about the quest of the Wise Men, he and the whole city were "greatly troubled."

After Herod had consulted with the Scribes about the prophecies concerning the Messiah, he invited the Wise Men to his palace, so he could question them and find out what they knew. Herod lied about wanting to worship the new baby king; he only wanted to discover his location. He planned on eliminating his future political opponent, just like many politicians do today.

When the Wise Men left Herod, they once again saw the star and were filled with joy. They followed the star to the adjacent town of Bethlehem, where it stopped and hovered over the house of Joseph, Mary, and the little boy Jesus. The fact that this star led the Wise Men to a specific location and stopped is evidence that this star was a special creation and not the aligning of planets or stars.

APPLICATION

The star is not an insignificant part of the Christmas Past Drama nor is it an insignificant part of the Christmas Future Drama. For many millennia, travelers on the land and sea have looked to the stars for guidance and direction, with the North Star as a fixed point of reference. It was fitting therefore that these travelers had a "Miracle Star" to lead and guide them to the "Miracle Child."

I believe the revelation God is releasing through this story is for those hungry souls who are truly seeking the face of their Messiah. I pray that a supernatural star will enlighten their paths and lead them to where they may find Him. How often could all of us have used that same star to guide us to the place where God would have us? People are always looking to God for guidance for the following:

- Where does God want me?
- Where should I work or study?
- What career should I pursue?
- Who should I marry?
- Where should I live?
- How should I invest my money?

Christmas Future

The most important thing when seeking God's guidance about your purpose in His plan is that you have pure heart motives. Ask yourself, are you actually just seeking Him to help you become successful and prosperous? It's not that He doesn't want you to be successful or prosperous, He's more interested in your heart and the motives behind that request. What He does promise is that those who truly seek first His Kingdom and His righteousness or justice, all these other things will be added unto them (Matthew 6:33). He embodies the true riches!

The Wise Men from Christmas Past were of one mind and heart when they heard about the new King being born. They already had great wealth and success. What they wanted was the opportunity to see the face of the Eternal One, born of a human mother, but also the Son of God. Their desire was to fall down and worship Him!

David, the man after God's own heart, frequently asked God to search his heart. He was first a worshiper, then a warrior, and finally a king who never lost a battle. David ended up an extremely blessed, wealthy and a powerful king of kings over the neighboring nations. What an example for us to follow! From intimacy in worship, asking God to search his heart, to fighting to defend God's reputation and protect His people, culminating in being given the honor of becoming the ruler of nations.

In this drama we call Christmas Future, I believe God will supernaturally soften the hearts of many who long to be in His presence to worship Him. Subsequently, the blessings of wealth and power will be granted to many such worshippers because God knows He can trust them with the authority of Heaven.

We Three Kings, Star of the East

Remember that Christmas Past was not the Really Big Event. It was a very special event that began the process that led to the Really Big Event. Even so, Christmas Future is not the Really Big Event. It is a very special event that also leads to the Really Big Event - the Glorious Return of King Jesus!

In this chapter, we have explored the concept of kings, wise men, and the star of Bethlehem. Let's transition now to another interesting feature of Christmas Past and its application to Christmas Future.

Silent Night

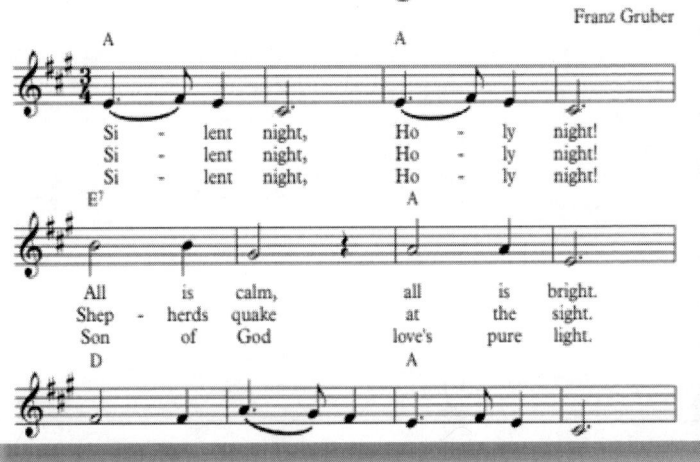

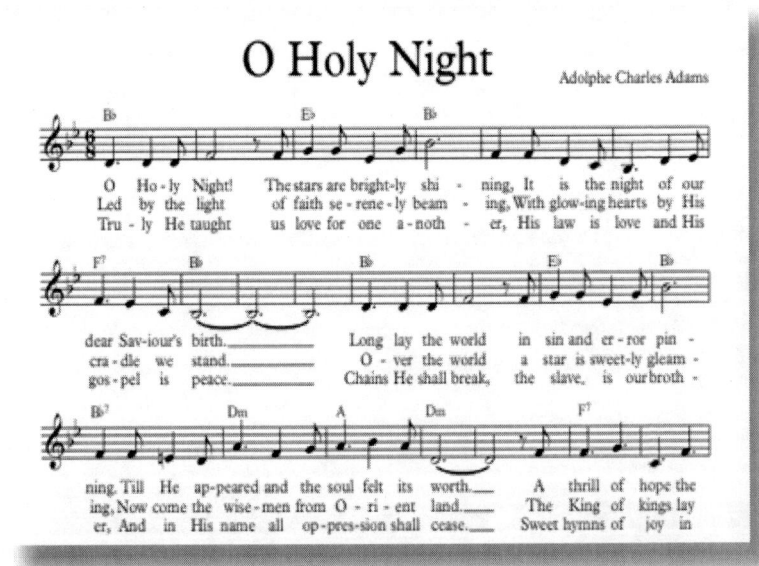

Franz Gruber

Si - lent night, Ho - ly night!
Si - lent night, Ho - ly night!
Si - lent night, Ho - ly night!
All is calm, all is bright.
Shep - herds quake at the sight.
Son of God love's pure light.

O Holy Night

Adolphe Charles Adams

O Ho-ly Night! The stars are bright-ly shi - ning, It is the night of our
Led by the light of faith se - rene-ly beam - ing, With glow-ing hearts by His
Tru - ly He taught us love for one a - noth - er, His law is love and His

dear Sav-iour's birth. Long lay the world in sin and er - ror pin -
cra - dle we stand. O - ver the world a star is sweet-ly gleam -
gos - pel is peace. Chains He shall break, the slave is our broth -

ning. Till He ap-peared and the soul felt its worth. A thrill of hope the
ing, Now come the wise-men from O - ri - ent land. The King of kings lay
er, And in His name all op-pres-sion shall cease. Sweet hymns of joy in

CHAPTER FIVE

SILENT NIGHT, O HOLY NIGHT

Two of the most famous Christmas carols are "Silent Night" and "O Holy Night." At first, I wasn't sure how to relate these titles to Christmas Future. But after prayer (my own and those of another intercessor), the revelation began to flow, and I'm very excited to share it with you.

Night involves darkness, and darkness usually symbolizes evil and danger. We usually sleep in darkness, and when we sleep, we are very vulnerable. "The valley of the shadow of death" is written about in Psalm 23. Shadows speak of limited light, and David puts forth the obvious danger lurking in those shadows, yet he feared no evil. Jesus added, *"Men loved darkness rather than light, because their deeds were evil"* (John 3:19b). In addition, there are numerous references to the dangers of walking in darkness and the difficulty of being able to

Silent Night, O Holy Night

accomplish much in the darkness. We are exhorted to work during the day, while we have light, because night is quickly approaching when we will be unable to work.

Thus, we have the issue of what makes a special night Holy or Silent? I believe God has a very special word for His people as we begin to celebrate Christmas Future. Let's begin in Isaiah 60:

Isaiah 60:1:
"Arise, shine; For your light has come! And the glory of the Lord is risen upon you."

Isaiah 60:2:
"For behold, the darkness shall cover the earth, and deep darkness the people; but the Lord will arise over you, and His glory will be seen upon you."

Isaiah 60:3:
"The Gentiles shall come to your light, and kings to the brightness of your rising."

It has often been said, "A little light shines brightest in total darkness." Isaiah speaks about "deep darkness." That's like being a mile into a cave tunnel and turning off your flashlight and all other artificial light. That's deep darkness!

When Jesus came to earth in Christmas Past, we must realize how great the spiritual darkness was in Israel. It had been four hundred years since the last prophetic writer had passed. The religious leaders exercised complete control over the spiritual lives of the people, and there was nothing left but religious ritual. Jesus became the Light of Life when He entered this world of spiritual darkness. Multitudes were attracted to Jesus

Christmas Future

upon seeing a truly bright light for the first time in their lifetimes.

Today, as we enter Christmas Future, the darkness is widespread, and it permeates almost every facet of our lives. We have seen darkness increase in education, government, media, family values, arts and entertainment, the financial world, and the religious institutions. Both Protestant and Roman Catholic leaders have accepted the debauchery that has been imposed on us by evil activists in our culture. We are seeing the powers of darkness being emboldened by victory after victory, and they have thrown all caution to the wind, going for the throat of their righteous enemies.

BUT GOD!

Isaiah 60:1 commands us to arise and shine because our Light has come. This is exactly what happened when Jesus invaded the darkness in a powerful way. We see such a beautiful and strategic assault on the powers of darkness in the days of Jesus and the beloved Christmas Past story.

ANGELS AND SHEPHERDS

The faithful shepherds were watching over their flocks by night, protecting them during the darkness. Suddenly, the darkness was pierced by the floodlight radiating from the "Angel of the Lord." How awesome that must have been! But even more awesome was when the entire sky was illuminated by the "multitude of the heavenly host."

By appearing at night, the angels were a prophetic sign that Baby Jesus had come to be the Light of the World. Yes, they were in a time of spiritual darkness, but God was sending a very bright light.

That powerful light was a sign that their long night of spiritual darkness was over. It was also a sign to the shepherds that they were not in any danger that night. There was a great army of God's warring angels surrounding their field, and no evil entity would be allowed to harass them.

THE WISE MEN

When God created the universe, as recorded in Genesis 1, He created the sun to rule by day and the moon and stars to rule by night. The night would not be completely dark because the moon and stars emitted light. Thus, it was fitting that these Wise Men, from a nation with very little spiritual light, found guidance from a lesser light in the sky known as "The Star of Bethlehem." The starlight was dim compared to the sun, but it was bright enough to guide the Wise Men to the brightest point in the universe - the Son of God. Without the darkness of night, they would not have been able to see that special star.

Jesus directed us to be the "light of the world." With greater darkness, our opportunity to be that light is only increased, and that's the greatest thing about Christmas, whether it's in the past or future. There was and is and will be a wonderful opportunity to shine God's light deep into the darkness. In Isaiah 60:3, we are told that this light, which will be seen shining from us, will draw many others to the Light of God. Even kings and rulers will be drawn to that Light.

This is not a small or minor point. This is God's greatest strategy for evangelism. This is what happened at Pentecost and what

Christmas Future

has happened during every great revival in history. People from all walks of life will spend time, money, and energy to get to a revival where God is moving. There is a hunger deep inside the heart of every human being to connect with a supernatural God.

And it all starts when the darkness is the deepest and God sends His light to this planet. Are you ready to shine that light into a dark world? Are you ready to be a lighthouse to those lost at sea?

SILENT NIGHT

The most sung Christmas carol over the past century or so is probably "Silent Night." The words do have significance, although it took a little meditation, followed by revelation. The meaning and application of the words "Silent Night" applies to both Christmas Past and Christmas Future.

What was so silent about that eventful night? Certainly, the angels weren't silent, nor were the shepherds after hearing their message. In the manger, we can assume that Mary did some groaning in the natural delivery that took place, and Joseph surely was coaching her on when to breathe and push. We should also assume that Baby Jesus, as holy as He was, still cried as He took His first breath. And we can't rule out some of the animal noises in the stable; the odd hee-haw of the donkeys, the mooing of the cows, and the bleating of the sheep may have punctuated the silence from time to time.

What then made it a "silent night?" I believe it was a "holy hush" in the spirit realm. Even as Mary silently pondered in her heart what she had heard, I suspect the attending angels and the fearful demons in the land were all at a loss for words, other than what was spoken by the angels to the shepherds that night. The demonic legions must have been struck dumb, knowing something terrible was happening to them. They were aware of the angel armies that had invaded the territory and expelled them from certain places where they normally had great freedom.

It was an especially silent night for their evil leader, who was blindsided by the secret timing of this event. Even the wisest Scribes and Pharisees who knew where it would happen totally missed out on participating in the great Christmas Past drama because they didn't know when it would happen.

Just as the angels shut the mouths of the lions when Daniel was thrown into their den, they shut the mouths of the enemies of the King of kings and Lord of lords who was born that blessed night.

APPLICATION

I am boldly predicting that the power of God to silence the voice of the adversary will be beautifully revealed in Christmas Future in a way that our generation has never seen before. What this means is:

- When God's light shines into the darkness of a generation hooked on drugs in massive revival meetings, the demonic forces behind those drugs will be silenced. The Holy Spirit will convict and deliver them from the power of this stronghold in mass deliverance miracles.

- When God's light shines into the darkness of a generation that has been taught the demonic lie of evolution, the lying educators, both demonic and human, will be silenced. The Holy Spirit will remove the veil of deception and reveal the truth about Creation.

- When God's light shines into the darkness of a generation seduced into a totally immoral lifestyle, those demons of lust and pornography will be silenced. The Holy Spirit will reveal the beauty of God's plan for biblical morality.

- And there will be much more silencing of demonic powers happening during the great times of deliverance in the season of Christmas Future. This is something to get excited about! Imagine being in the angelic atmosphere of God's glory where there was no evil voice tempting you to sin. Perhaps you've experienced that during times of revival, where you felt totally surrendered to God with no desire to do anything that wouldn't please Him. But then you left that atmosphere and had to deal with a world of darkness, and the temptations started to return. Christmas Future will expand that glorious atmosphere, and it will go with you wherever you go, silencing the voice of your adversary. What an exciting thought!

OH, HOLY NIGHT

The word "Holy" means set aside, or dedicated, for a special purpose. This night had been on God's secret calendar for some time. It was truly a night set aside from all other nights, and it was dedicated by God for a special purpose. What began as a typical night filled with darkness was soon revealed not to be in

Silent Night, O Holy Night

any way ordinary. To those whom God chose, it was a night to be remembered forever.

It was an extremely holy night, especially for one important reason. It was the first and only time in recorded history that a woman carried a child in her womb who was the one and only eternal Son of God. It was that special night for birthing this heavenly baby, who grew up calling Himself the Son of Man. It was the launching of the Ship of Salvation, which would culminate in The Really Big Event - The Crucifixion and Resurrection of the Son of God.

While Christmas Future is not a one-day event, it will be a Holy Season of great and unprecedented spiritual blessing, bringing us incredible joy and fulfillment. And that's a great transition to our next chapter.

Joy To The World
Isacc Watts
Handel
A E/A D/A A Bm/D A/E E7 A A/C♯
1. Joy to the world! The Lord is come; Let
2. Joy to the earth! The Sav - ior reigns; Let
3. No more let sins and sor - rows grow, nor
4. He rules the world with truth and grace, and
5
D E A D/A A
earth re - ceive her King; Let ev - 'ry
men their songs em - ploy; While field and
thorns in - fest the ground; He comes to
makes the na - tions prove the glo - ries
9
D/A A
heart pre - pare Him room. And heav'n and na - ture
floods, rocks, hills and plains, re - peat the sound-ing
make His bless - ings flow far as the curse is
of His righ - eous - ness. And won-ders of His
13
E E7 A/E E
sing, and heav'n and na - ture sing. And
joy, re - peat the sound - ing joy. Re -
found, far as the curse is found. Far
love, and won - ders of His love. And
16
A D/A A Bm/D A/E E7 A
heav'n and heav'n and na - ture sing.
-peat, re - peat the sound - ing joy.
as, far as, the curse is found.
won - ders, won - ders of His love.
©MichaelKravchuk.com

CHAPTER 6

JOY TO THE WORLD

Christmas Past was punctuated with announcements and expressions of raw and authentically pure joy. I totally expect the same experience in even greater measure during Christmas Future.

We've read about the promise of joy and rejoicing in the all of the Christmas Past passages. In Matthew 2:10, *"When they* (the Wise Men) *saw the star, they rejoiced with exceedingly great joy."* In Luke 1:14, Gabriel spoke to Zacharias about John, *"You will have joy and gladness, and many will rejoice at his birth."*

In Luke 1:28a, Gabriel told Mary, *"Rejoice, highly favored one."* In Luke 1:44, Elizabeth, pregnant with John, explained to Mary, who was visiting and pregnant with Jesus, *"For indeed, as soon as the voice of your greeting sounded in my ears, the babe leaped in my womb for joy."*

What a powerful moment, with such great applications! In Luke 2:10b, the Angel of the Lord delivered those famous words, *"Behold, I bring you good tidings of great joy, which will be to all people."*

In addition to these Christmas Past references, there are many passages throughout the Old and New Testaments that speak of the joy that comes to those who love and follow Jesus, especially when He manifests His presence in power and love. When Jesus shows up on the scene and begins to perform powerful miracles, the joy juices flow like the most beautiful fountains this world has ever seen!

Church history also records numerous revivals or Great Awakenings. Yes, many of these revivals have been marked by agonizing sorrow at the altar, as people cried out to God and repented of their sins. However, we also read that when the breakthrough came, they experienced incredible joy. I've also experienced this revival and joy in my seventy plus years on this earth.

My greatest personal revival occurred in my freshman year at Canadian Bible College in Regina, the capital city of Saskatchewan, Canada. It began with the conviction of my self-centeredness and lack of burden for others, which I confessed to my college classmates. That confession supernaturally developed into months of deep intercession for the church of Jesus. I'd spend an hour or two every morning before and sometimes during breakfast, weeping over the lukewarmness of the church with a deep, deep cry for revival. I was reading through the Book of Acts every two days. While kneeling at a piano bench in a small piano practice room, I cried out to God, "Please wake up your church. We are a sleeping giant with

Christmas Future

incredible power available to us that we're not using. Please Lord, do again what you did in the book of Acts."

When the intercessory burden began to lift after an hour or two, an incredible euphoria of absolute and blissful joy would flood my spirit. This happened day after day for several months. My daily mourning over the condition of the church was turned into daily unspeakable joy. This was the fruit of the Holy Spirit, unavailable to those who seek joy from any earthly source.

It was only a few years later that a wonderful revival came to our city. It went on for six solid weeks, led by a revival team that had just spent eight amazing weeks in Saskatoon, Saskatchewan. That Canadian Revival in the early 1970's was also filled with the sorrow of repentance, followed by incredible joy. Held in a large church facility, the non-denominational revival had very little preaching but a lot of prayer and personal testimonies. Those testimonies created hunger in those who were coming to check it out. Evening services usually lasted until around 11 PM or midnight, but the afterglows, as they called them, went further into the night.

I remember seeing teenagers and parents hugging and apologizing to one another with tears of joy running down their faces. That kind of joy cannot be faked with religious ceremonies and traditions. The revival was also characterized by many people returning goods they had taken from work, while others refiled income taxes because of the cheating they had done. Every act of obedience was rewarded with more joy from Heaven. After six weeks, there were calls coming in from city after city and the revival team began to move on. Meanwhile, some of the leaders who had been a part of the revival also began to travel, enabling the revival to spread more quickly.

But the Canadian revival was just an appetizer for this young man. I was anxious to see more of the book of Acts restored to the church. While the Canadian revival was the greatest move of God I had ever experienced, it didn't feature much in the way of healings or other supernatural manifestations of God's power, and there weren't a large number of salvations recorded. It was a revival to revive and purify the church. Because many of the participating churches were not very open to the manifestations of the Holy Spirit, there were few physical miracles, resulting in few salvations.

In 1973, I was invited to accompany an older pastor/evangelist named E. R. Burnette to do meetings in the nation of Argentina. I had gotten to know Pastor Burnette and had assisted in his ministry in Albany, Oregon. A former associate of his named Jack Schissler had become a missionary there. He was in fellowship with several local pastors in various cities, and he had also started a small Bible School in the city of Cordoba. Jack Schissler was a passionate worshiper and his students mostly followed in his footsteps. He felt it was time to invite a man to Argentina who flowed in the gifts of healing, deliverance, knowledge, and prophecy.

By this time, I had married Brenda Pinkerton, a precious and beautiful girl from Seattle, who took a chance on a radical Canadian kid who wanted to live by faith. We also had one child named Kenneth, who was about eighteen months old. Plus, we took care of another six-year-old, also named Ken. Brenda was a few months pregnant with our second baby, whom we decided to name Barbara. No, it wasn't on purpose that we had

Christmas Future

a Barbie and Ken. Others soon noticed their names and didn't miss the opportunity to tease them about it. They were actually named Kenneth and Barbara after family members.

Brenda spent six weeks with her family and two kids in Seattle, while I journeyed on my first trip outside of North America. She bravely endured many difficult situations without my help, while I was having the most glorious time of my life. She deserves huge rewards for those six weeks, but she had no hesitation in affirming that I should travel with our beloved pastor.

In Argentina, we had meetings in several cities, but they all featured the same powerful miracles that I had prayed for back in the mid 1960's. The gifts of the Holy Spirit flowed unhindered. From the first night onward, we saw incredible miracles every meeting, and as a result, we saw over one thousand souls saved in those six weeks. The miracles the people saw and experienced, revealed the love and power of Jesus like nothing they had ever experienced. They wanted to know the Jesus that was doing all the miracles. Brother Burnette, as we called him, constantly reminded the people that he had no power in himself. It was Jesus doing all the miracles.

As a catalyst to many of the miracles that occurred during this time, the gift of knowledge was working powerfully with incredible visions, like HD videos, revealing to the people that God knew them and how much He cared about them. For instance, Brother Burnette saw a woman crying in her home because her husband was not a believer. The next night her husband came and accepted Jesus. Other times, God would show him what sickness certain people had and how many in an area had the same physical infirmity.

Some days he would see a preview of what would happen that night. I remember him saying that a young man would be there in a purple jacket and God was going to heal him. Of course, it happened just like he had seen it a few hours before. In every public meeting, we witnessed people being healed, saved, and filled with the Holy Spirit.

Starting the very first night, many were healed of cancer. One night two young men born deaf and dumb were healed and began to talk. Another night a young boy with the same condition was healed. Many with vision problems were also healed. I held a small child with club feet and watched as they straightened out. Tears of joy flowed down the mother's face.

In the town of La Falda, the not-yet-Christian hotel owners, where the meetings were held, were observing us praying over people, and they consented to receive prayer for themselves. It was revealed that the wife had crippling arthritis and couldn't open and close her hands. Her fingers were frozen in a curled-up position. As we prayed for a miracle, she began to open and close her hands. She and her husband both began to weep with incredible joy. Saying that it was easy to get them to accept Jesus as Savior and Lord would have been the understatement of the year. Their lives were forever changed to the glory of God!

JOY IN MORE RECENT REVIVALS

Joy was the word that best described the various manifestations that occurred during the "Toronto Blessing" revival, which began in 1994. Thousands of people from all over the world made the journey to Toronto, Ontario, Canada, to get in on a very unusual move of God. It was like nothing anyone had ever experienced before. The laughter was extremely contagious. People would look at someone that just got hit with laughter, often rolling on the floor, and it would get them laughing. For many, it was the first time they had ever laughed in church, but along with the laughter came visitations and inner healing.

Proverbs 17:22a:
"A merry heart does good, like a medicine."

On the heels of the Toronto Blessing revival came the Brownsville revival in Pensacola, Florida. This revival was definitely a different flavor, but joy was still a dominant feature of this movement.

Without belaboring the point, suffice it to say that when the Holy Spirit moves on God's people, the fruit of the Spirit always manifests. The second fruit mentioned after love is joy.

When Jesus came into the world two thousand years ago, the angels promised great joy to all people. Very few participated in that joy in the beginning, but later they obtained a great salvation provided by the Savior of the World. When they received the infilling of the Holy Spirit, they experienced the joy that has been spreading to every corner of the world. Joy will always be a trademark of the presence of God in our midst, even in the midst of pain and suffering.

Rolland and Heidi Baker, founders of Iris Ministries based in Mozambique, have reported unbelievable stories of native Christians who were attacked and persecuted by people of other religions. And yet, when they worship in God's presence, they can overcome the pain of seeing their loved ones tortured

Joy To The World

and killed. The Bakers testify that these persecuted saints actually manifest unspeakable joy in their worship. The joy they experience is healing medicine for their broken hearts.

We've seen in this chapter many examples, both from Scripture and from church history, of the joy that resulted from Christmas Past. I strongly and firmly believe that we will see that kind of joy and more as we participate in Christmas Future.

We come now to our final Christmas carol, with a prayer for God to visit us again with His glorious and powerful presence.

O Come, O Come Emmanuel

O come, O come Emmanuel, And ransom captive Israel, That mourns in lonely exile here, Until the Son of God appear. Rejoice, rejoice! Emmanuel shall come to Thee, O Israel!

O come, Thou Rod of Jesse, free, Thine own from Satan's tyranny, From depths of Hell Thy people save, And give them vict'ry o'er the grave. Rejoice, rejoice! Emmanuel shall come to Thee, O Israel!

O come, Thou Day-Spring, come and cheer, Our spirits by Thine advent here, Disperse the gloomy clouds of night, And death's dark shadows put to flight. Rejoice, rejoice! Emmanuel shall come to Thee, O Israel!

©MichaelKravchuk.com

CHAPTER SEVEN

O COME, O COME EMMANUEL

"Behold, the virgin shall be with child, and bear a Son, and they shall call His name Immanuel," which is translated, *"God with us"* (Matthew 1:23).

"Therefore the Lord Himself will give you a sign: Behold, the virgin shall conceive and bear a Son, and shall call His name Immanuel" (Isaiah 7:14).

Matthew quotes Isaiah 7:14, after he describes the angelic visit to Joseph. This is an amazing messianic prophecy, which is well-known in Christian circles.

As I write this today, I feel God's heart crying out to His people. "This is not just a great Christmas carol. If only My people knew how I long to respond to the prayer of this song! I created you to be a people I could dwell among and with whom I could share My goodness. I want to always be that loving Father who can answer your questions and bless you with My wisdom. I want to show you My miracle power when you get into trouble, and I want to surprise you with special blessings every day of your lives. I do want to come and be with you. You'll never know how much My heart longs for that. Even now, I am drawing many people into My heart. They are hearing My heartbeat for the first time, even as My disciple John did when he leaned upon My chest. I'm inviting you also to join them and experience a deeper devotion to Me, while I reveal My undying love to you."

It was the greatest miracle of Christmas Past. The actual Son of God came to earth in human form, calling Himself the Son of Man. He was Emmanuel, God with us, for at least thirty-three years. It was a miracle of unprecedented proportions. There had been a number of visitations to men like Abraham, Moses, and Joshua, but there was never anything like the Son of God growing up and living among men as the true Emmanuel. It was the by far the greatest ultimate expression of love that this world has ever seen!

The previous chapter focused on the second fruit of the Holy Spirit, the Spirit of Joy. This final chapter will focus on the first fruit of the Holy Spirit, which is the Spirit of Love. Without love, there is no real joy, but with God's divine Agape Love, there is no limitation on our joy.

Watch how Jesus sandwiched "fullness of joy" between these powerful verses on love:

John 15:9-10:
"As the Father loved Me, I also have loved you; abide in My love. If you keep my commandments, you will abide in My love, just as I have kept My Father's commandments and abide in His love."

John 15:11:
"These things have I spoken to you, that My joy may remain in you, and that your joy may be full."

John 15:12-13:
"This is My commandment, that you love one another as I have loved you. Greater love has no one than this, than to lay down one's life for his friends."

We know that Jesus was setting the bar high for them so they would fail in their own strength. Jesus knew they would fail, even though they thought they were strong enough not to. He wanted them to experience their weakness so that He could infuse them with supernatural strength. After the cross and His resurrection, the power of the Holy Spirit would be released in their lives. The disciples did not yet possess God's supernatural Agape Love, but they soon would.

We must also understand that we are only weak humans, and our strong determination is not enough to produce supernatural love. We desperately need God's miracle love to invade our lives in every relationship. We need The Marriage Anointing (another book title), to properly love our mate, and we certainly need an anointing of grace to love our enemies.

What we need is Emmanuel – God with us and in us. Jesus made it clear to His disciples how important it was for Him to return to His Father so that the Holy Spirit could dwell with them as the representative of Jesus. He is also our Emmanuel for the present time.

The Holy Spirit puts the cry in our hearts so that we're dissatisfied with our situation as it is. He wants us to cry, "Maranatha! – Come Lord Jesus." While the Holy Spirit is God and powerful, He points us to Jesus; He doesn't come to glorify Himself. Jesus, or Yeshua, is our only Savior and coming King. He will come again in human form and reveal His glory and power for all to see.

The coming of Jesus at Christmas Past was wonderful and the launching of something amazing, but it was not the Really Big Event. As shared earlier, that event was the crucifixion and resurrection of our Savior and Lord. Likewise, Pentecost was a powerful transformative experience, and every unique revival of the past has touched hearts and changed lives. Christmas Future is going to be amazing! But neither Christmas Past, nor Christmas Future can compare with The Really, Really, Really Big Event.

That Great and World-Transforming Event will be "The Glorious Return of King Jesus." It will bring true justice, punish evil-doers, reward righteousness, and establish a Kingdom of Peace and Love for one thousand years!

THE PROPHETIC INTERCESSORS OF CHRISTMAS PAST AND FUTURE

There are two more, often overlooked, yet very important characters with a special role in the Christmas Past Drama. Their stories are recorded in Luke 2:25-38. Both of these individuals would have loved the theme hymn of this chapter.

Christmas Future

They truly lived for the coming of the Messiah and King, their Emmanuel.

The first individual, given the most print space in Scripture, was named Simeon. Please read the following verses with a sensitive heart, so as not to miss the voice of the Holy Spirit speaking to you.

Luke 2:25:
"And behold, there was a man in Jerusalem whose name was Simeon, and this man was just and devout, waiting for the Consolation of Israel, and the Holy Spirit was upon him."

Luke 2:26:
"And it had been revealed to him by the Holy Spirit that he would not see death before he had seen the Lord's Christ."

Luke 2:27-32:
"So he came by the Spirit into the temple. And when the parents brought in the Child Jesus, to do for Him according to the custom of the law, he took Him up in his arms and blessed God and said: 'Lord, now You are letting Your servant depart in peace, According to Your word; For my eyes have seen Your salvation Which you have prepared before the face of all peoples, A light to bring revelation to the Gentiles, and the glory of Your people Israel.'"

These eight verses should challenge us all to the core as we look forward to Christmas Future. As far as we know, this man was not a priest, like Zacharias, or of the lineage of King David. He was simply described as a "man in Jerusalem." We read of no special pedigree that made him eligible for preferential

O Come, O Come Emmanuel

treatment, which means that we don't need a special pedigree either to find favor with God.

We are told he was "just and devout, waiting for the Consolation of Israel." In other words, he was fervently praying, "O come, O come, Emmanuel." As I write this, I reflect on what I shared in the previous chapter. As a youth just out of high school, my personal passion was to pray that same prayer. I longed for Jesus to visit His church once again. I wanted to see His miracle-working power and His incomprehensible and passionate love for us freely on display.

Then we read the comment, *"And the Holy Spirit was upon him."* Oh Lord Jesus, may those words also be spoken about me and those who read this book. Because of Simeon's devotion to God, it was revealed to him that he would not see death until He had seen the Lord's Christ - the Anointed One from Heaven. It's another proof that God reveals His secrets to those who truly love Him, as opposed to the intellectual scholars, who have no intimate relationship with Him.

I love verse 27: *"So he came by the Spirit into the temple."* Jesus would later be led by the Spirit into the wilderness. But in this special moment of Christmas Past, it's just a man with a heart for God who was led by the Spirit. Simeon came into the temple, the place of God's presence, and began to pray and prophesy under a special anointing.

Notice now verses 33-35.

Luke 2:33:
"And Joseph and His mother marveled at those things which were spoken of Him."

Christmas Future

Luke 2:34:
"Then Simeon blessed them, and said to Mary His mother, 'Behold this Child is destined for the fall and rising of many in Israel, and for a sign which will be spoken against (yes, a sword will pierce through your own soul also), that the thoughts of many hearts may be revealed.'"

These prophetic words point to the sacrifice of Jesus on the cross, piercing the soul of Mary. Simeon also prophesied that the hearts of many of the religious leaders would be exposed for their hypocrisy and pride of position.

We could spend more time with Simeon's role in this drama, but let us look at one final player, who deserves our admiration. Her name was Anna. Let's read Luke 2:36-38.

Luke 2:36:
"Now there was one Anna, a prophetess, the daughter of Phanuel, of the tribe of Asher. She was of a great age, and had lived with a husband seven years from her virginity;"

Luke 2:37:
"And this woman was a widow of about eighty-four years, who did not depart from the temple, but served God with fastings and prayers night and day."

Luke 2:38:
"And coming in that instant she gave thanks to the Lord, and spoke of Him to all those who looked for redemption in Jerusalem."

O Come, O Come Emmanuel

We are told of Anna that she was of the tribe of Asher. Asher was not a very prominent tribe, but Anna didn't let that stop her from being a prophetic intercessor. She was probably well past one hundred years old, having been married ninety-one years before Jesus was brought into the temple.

Being a prophetess, she had probably been sensing the soon coming of their Messiah. When Simeon was speaking and prophesying to Mary, Anna walked into the temple, and she began to praise and worship God for allowing her to see the baby Jesus also. She had most likely been singing *O Come, O Come, Emmanuel* in Hebrew for many years.

APPLICATION

These final characters in the Christmas Past Drama are such a powerful challenge to us who look for Christmas Future to manifest.

Amos 3:7:
"Surely the Lord God does nothing, Unless He reveals His secret to His servants the prophets."

Simeon and Anna were true prophetic intercessors. They prepared the way for John the Baptist, who also helped them prepare the way for Jesus. In our world today, God has truly raised up many Simeons and Annas. There are multitudes of incredibly dedicated prophetic intercessors, who are crying out day and night with fastings, that Jesus would visit His church with revival. They are praying for the full manifestation of what I call Christmas Future. They know that it's time to bring in the initial harvest and to prepare the bride of Christ for His coming.

Christmas Future

We are all invited to participate to some degree in prophetic intercession. We may not all be called to be prophets or prophetesses, but we can all be anointed intercessors with a prophetic edge to touch the hearts of others and to move the hand of God. He responds to the cries of His people, and He acts when they make their voices heard in Heaven.

O COME, O COME, EMMANUEL!

This world is a mess. We need a righteous king to rule over us. We need to stop the wars and greed of evil men. We need to have demonic doctrines extracted from our religious institutions, our education systems, our governments, etc.

Please come, Lord Jesus, and establish your Kingdom on this earth. We thank you for Christmas Past and Christmas Future. We know Christmas Future will be a wonderful season to bring in Your harvest and prepare Your bride. But we long for that deeper, more personal, and intimate relationship with the Son of God, whom we can behold and touch with human hands on this earth.
 O COME, O COME, EMMANUEL!!!!

FINAL THOUGHTS AND SUMMARY

We have been examining the first Christmas, when Jesus was born in Bethlehem, and we refer to it as Christmas Past. We are discovering how prophetic it is relative to what we are calling Christmas Future, which is partially based on what many prophetic people have proclaimed for decades about the days ahead. They haven't called it Christmas Future, as I have, but they believe a great world-wide harvest of souls is about to take place. What I believe God has been showing me is that it will be very similar or parallel to Christmas Past in many ways. Drawing from this insight, we are also predicting many great blessings will accompany the manifestations of Jesus on the earth before His great, awesome, and visible return, where every eye shall see Him - the really, Really, REALLY big event.

These great blessings and manifestations will include:

1. Many servants of God will become like the manger or feeding trough of Christmas Past. They will feed hungry souls and provide a humble dwelling place in their hearts where their Messiah can rest and dwell.

2. Angelic activity will greatly increase. People will have dreams, visions, and incredible encounters with angels.

3. Shepherds (pastors) will have greater sacrificial love for their people and watch over them (like David) in their times of greatest danger. They will also be quick to investigate moves of God, as they hear of them, with hungry hearts.

4. There will be kings and wise men who come to worship Jesus, wherever He can be found. They will have wealth to enrich His Kingdom, and they will have the Spirit of wisdom to help build it. They will interact with the angelic realm and be obedient to their instructions, just like the humble shepherds.

5. The light from the armies of Heaven will drive out the demonic forces trying to keep people in darkness. Their evil, forked tongues will be silenced, and their power to

control people during this time will be decimated. Many prodigals will be freed from demonic control and will return to their families and their God.

6. A new level of great joy will be witnessed among the saints of God and in those who are turning to their Savior and Lord for the first time. It will be "joy unspeakable and full of glory."

7. The glorious manifestations of revival, awakening, reformation and the great and final harvest will produce a common cry among the children of God declaring, "O COME, O COME, EMMANUEL!"

EVEN SO, COME LORD JESUS! **(Revelation 22:20)**

PRAYER

If you have never experienced the love and the joy of a personal relationship with God, and you've never invited Jesus into your life to become His child and disciple, it's really not that complicated. You can talk to God in your own words and say something like this:

Dear Jesus, I choose to acknowledge you as my Lord and Savior. I believe you died to save me. I'm sorry for all my sins. I've lived for myself, but now I want to live for You. I want to serve you and help build Your Kingdom and tell others about Your love for me.

I also ask you to fill me to overflowing with Your Holy Spirit. I need the power to live for You and to reveal Your love to others. Please anoint me with the supernatural fruit and gifts that were given to Your disciples.

O Come, O Come Emmanuel

Thank You, Jesus, for saving me and giving me a new life in You. Teach me Your ways and lead me into Your truth. Help me to understand Your Holy Words as recorded in the Bible. In Your wonderful and holy name, I pray! Amen!

Ben R. Peters

Ben R. Peters has been a student of the Word since he could read it for himself. He has a heritage of grandparents and parents who lived by faith and taught him the value of faith. That faith produced many miracle answers to prayer in their family life, as Ben and his wife, Brenda, have shared over 55 years of marriage and gospel ministry. Together they founded Kingdom Sending Center, in northern Illinois, and travel extensively, teaching and ministering prophetically to thousands each year. Their books are available on most e-readers, all other normal book outlets, as well as their website: www.kingdomsendingcenter.org.

Other Books Written by Ben R. Peters:

1. A Mandate to Laugh
2. Birthing the Book Within You
3. The Boaz Blessing
4. Catching Up to the Third World
5. Cinco Ministeriors En Un Poderoso Equipo
6. Faith on Fire
7. Finding Your Place on Your Kingdom Mountain
8. Folding Five Ministries into One Powerful Team
9. God is So God!
10. God's Favorite Number
11. Go Ahead, Be So Emotional
12. Holy How?
13. Holy Passion – Desire on Fire
14. Humility and How I Almost Achieved It
15. The Kingdom-Building Church
16. Kings & Kingdoms
17. **The Glorious Return of King Jesus – New!**
18. The Marriage Anointing
19. Ministry Foundations 101
20. Prophetic Ministry -Strategic Key to the Harvest
21. Resurrection! A Manual for Raising the Dead
22. Signs and Wonders - To Seek or Not to Seek
23. The Ultimate Convergence
24. Veggie Village and the Great & Dangerous Jungle
25. With Me

A Mandate to Laugh

Overcoming the Sennacherib Spirit

In this book you will learn about the demonic power that possessed Sennacherib and how it is influencing our society and political powers today. The clear and sinister purpose of the Sennacherib spirit is to control all people and nations for personal glory, power, and profit. Yet, there is still hope God is not finished with the world!

Birthing the Book Within You

Inspiration and Practical Help to Produce Your Own Book

Writing and publishing your own book has never been easier, thanks to computer and digital printing technology. Ben R. Peters has been down this road many times, and now in this book, he shows how you can do it too. With spiritual insight and inspiration, he offers many practical tips to help you give birth to the book within you.

The Boaz Blessing

Releasing the Power of This Ancient Blessing Into Your World Today

The Boaz Blessing will give you courage as you dare to believe for the favor of God for yourself, for the people you love, and for the people who need to understand the mercy of their heavenly Father.

Catching Up to the Third World

Seven Indispensable Keys to Explosive Revival in the Western Church

Catching Up to the Third World reveals how God is provoking the Western Church to godly jealousy, to produce a powerful revival in the "First World" nations, so that the resources of the West can be most effectively utilized in the coming global harvest.

Cinco Ministerios En Un Poderoso Equipo

Llevando la Reforma Profetica y Apostolica Al Siguiente Nivel

Este libro da a la iglesia una visión de lo que podemos lograr cuando capacitamos a cada ministerio para hacer lo que mejor puede hacer como parte del equipo ministerial que Dios ha dado a la iglesia.

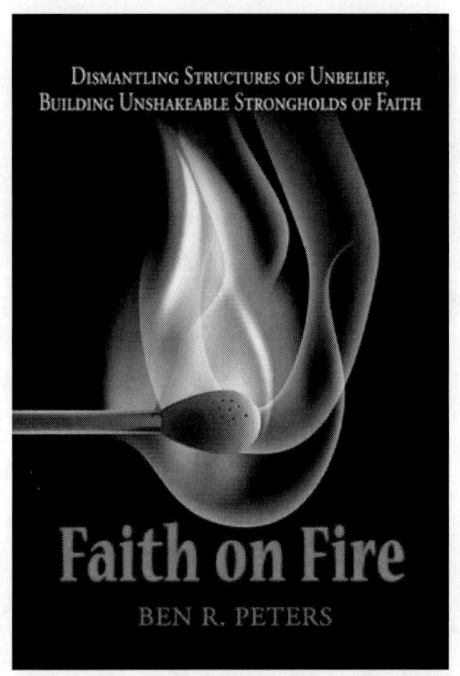

Faith on Fire

Dismantling Structures of Unbelief, Building Unshakeable Strongholds of Faith

Most Christians wonder why they don't see greater results from their prayers. In *Faith on Fire*, Ben R. Peters addresses these questions and identifies the structures of unbelief that may be keeping you in fear, doubt, and insecurity.

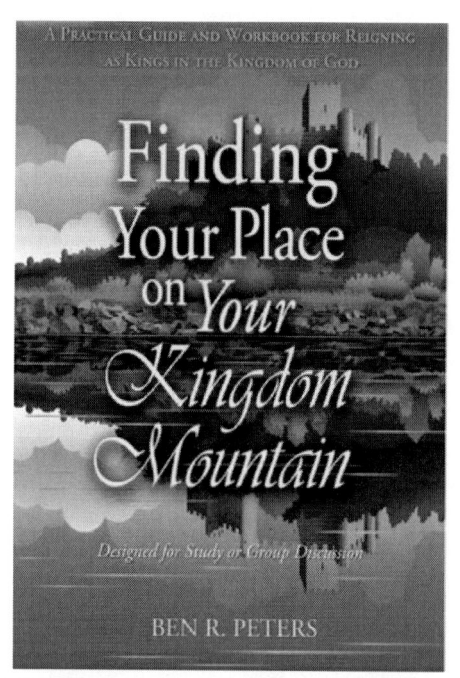

Finding Your Place on Your Kingdom Mountain

A Practical Guide and Workbook for Reigning as Kings in the Kingdom of God

In *Finding Your Place on Your Kingdom Mountain,* Ben R. Peters gives you practical help to discover on which of the "Seven Mountains" of society God wants you to display the rule and reign of His kingdom.

Folding Five Ministries into One Powerful Team

Taking the Apostolic and Prophetic Reformation to the Next Powerful Level

This book gives the Church a vision for what can be accomplished when we empower each ministry to do what it does best as part of the ministry team that God has given to the Church.

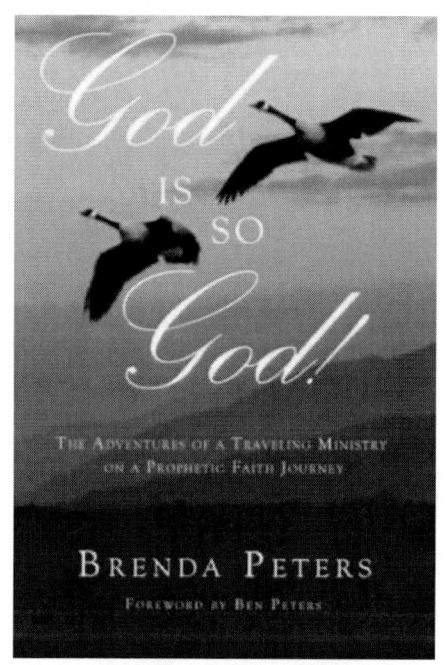

God is So God!

The Adventures of a Traveling Ministry on a Prophetic Faith Journey

Brenda Peters knows what it's like to launch out on a faith journey with only an RV for her home. This book, filled with her road adventures in a full-time traveling ministry, reveals the awesome power of God to intervene in every aspect of life. This is a unique book, full of faith stories and prophetic adventures that will touch your heart.

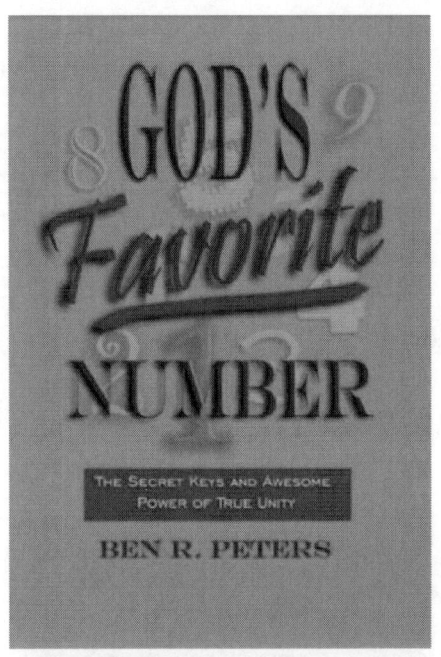

God's Favorite Number

The Secret Keys and
Awesome Power of True Unity

Does God have a favorite number? Yes, He does - so much so that you'll find it 1,969 times in Scripture. It's a number that relates to unity.

Go Ahead, Be So Emotional

Empowering <u>the</u> Emotional Personality
To <u>do</u> Awesome Exploits <u>for</u> God

It's time for all of God's emotionally expressive people to rise up and fulfill their destiny. In this book you will learn how to let the anointing of God come upon you as you use your emotional personality to take more territory for His kingdom.

Holy How?

Holiness, the Sabbath, Communion and Baptism

Enjoy the Privilege of Being Holy to the Lord! Believer, you are chosen to be special and unique and filled with the very nature of God, through your intimate relationship with the Father, Son, and Holy Spirit.

Holy Passion – Desire on Fire

Igniting The Torch of Godly Passion

God is a God of passion, and He is looking for a people with passion!

Humility and How I Almost Achieved It

UNCOVER A HIGHLY UNDERVALUED KEY TO LASTING SUCCESS AND KINGDOM POWER! You will learn the greatest shortcut to true humility, plus some practical ways to stay humble about being humble.

The Kingdom-Building Church

Experiencing the Explosive Potential of the Church in Kingdom-Building Mode

Come with Ben R. Peters and explore what the heart of God cries out for, what the plans of God are for His church, and what He can do when we allow Him to put us in Kingdom-building mode.

Kings and Kingdoms

Anointing A New Generation of Kings to Serve the King of Kings

In *Kings and Kingdoms*, Ben R. Peters explores what it means to be a king under the authority of Jesus Christ and how you can truly "seek first the Kingdom of God" by fulfilling your role as king over the domain God has given you.

Ben's Newest Book!

The Glorious Return of King Jesus

The Rapture and The Great Tribulation

Is there biblical evidence for a rapture? Is "Left Behind" an actual scriptural concept? Did God give us a type and shadow of His second coming in His Holy Word? This concise and easy-to-read investigation leaves little doubt what the answers to these and other questions are. You will love this unique journey!

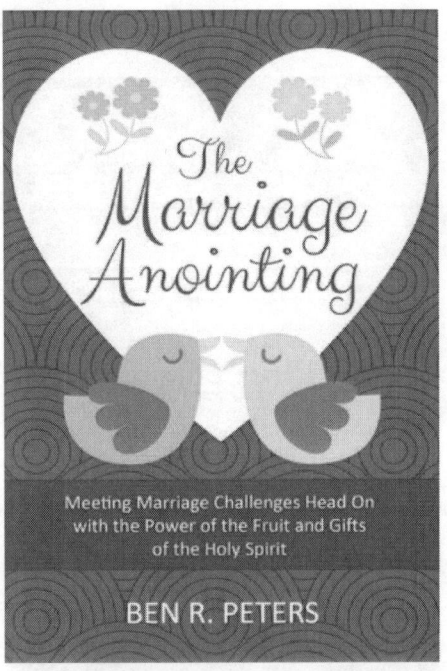

The Marriage Anointing

Meeting Marriage Challenges Head on with the Power of the Fruit and Gifts of the Holy Spirit

Meet your marriage challenges head on! There is no power from hell that can defeat *two* people who have learned to listen to God's voice and invite Him to bless them with everything He wants to bestow upon them. This book shows you how, with the "double-barreled" approach of the Fruit and Gifts of the Holy Spirit, your marriage can become a huge source of fulfillment for both partners and together become an awesome ministry team.

Ministry Foundations 101

Preparing the Saints for the Work of the Ministry

The goal of this study is to help you be the best possible stewards of the gifts, talents, knowledge, and experience that God has given to each of you.

PROPHETIC MINISTRY
Strategic Key to the Harvest

Ben R. Peters

Prophetic Ministry

Strategic Key to the Harvest

Ben R. Peters knows from first-hand experience the value and effectiveness of prophetic ministry as an evangelistic tool. Along with his wife Brenda, he has been doing prophetic ministry since 1999. He has seen countless salvations, healings, and miracles as a result.

Resurrection

A Manual for Raising the Dead

Let's Raise the Dead! Raising the dead is not for super-Christians but is in the DNA of every believer.

Signs and Wonders
To Seek or Not to Seek

Exploring The Power of the Miraculous to Bring People to Christ

To Seek or Not to Seek? Signs and Wonders gives a clear and resounding answer to that controversial question. The conclusions of this thorough and fascinating investigation of the faith-making power of the miraculous will be difficult to refute.

The Ultimate Convergence

An End Times Prophecy of the Greatest Shock and Awe Display Ever to Hit Planet Earth

Convergence has been a hot buzzword in Kingdom streams for the past few years. Ben R. Peters believes that God is preparing for the greatest convergence of natural and spiritual elements of all time in preparation for His great harvest and the coming back to earth of His Beloved Son, Jesus Christ.

Veggie Village and the Great & Dangerous Jungle: An Allegory

When church becomes more of a religion than a relationship, it can seem like just eating our vegetables. We are told to do good things like read our Bibles, pray, and go to church because they are good for us - and they are. However, God wants to win the lost, and it is often not easy to get others to come and eat with us if we offer only vegetables.

With Me

With Me takes you on an incredible journey of discovery about the Lord Jesus, as it uncovers a refreshing new revelation from the most famous Psalm in Scripture.

All Books are Available from Kingdom Sending Center
www.kingdomsendingcenter.org

Manufactured by Amazon.ca
Acheson, AB